THE OPEN MEDIA PAMPHLET SERIES

Zapatista Encuentro

Documents from the 1996 Encounter for Humanity and Against Neoliberalism

THE ZAPATISTAS

Series editors Greg Ruggiero and Stuart Sahulka

SEVEN STORIES PRESS / New York

A Seven Stories Press First Edition,
published in association with Open Media.

Open Media Pamphlet Series editors,
Greg Ruggiero and Stuart Sahulka.

Library of Congress Cataloging-in-Publication Data

   Zapatista Encuentro: documents from the 1996
Encounter for Humanity and against Neoliberalism
/ the Zapatistas. —A Seven Stories Press 1st ed.
   p.   cm. —(The Open Media Pamphlet Series)
   ISBN: 1-888363-58-4
   1. Chiapas (Mexico)—History—Peasant Upris-
ing, 1994–   —Congresses. 2. Ejército Zapatista de
Liberación Nacional (Mexico)—Congresses. I. Marcos, subcomandante. II. Ejército Zapatista de Liberación Nacional (Mexico). III. Title
F1256.Z26 1996
972.08′35—dc21   97-23150
                                  CIP

Book design by Cindy LaBreacht
9 8 7 6 5 4 3 2 1

The Zapatistas are an indigenous insurgency movement demanding political and economic democracy in Mexico. Their guerilla activity began on January 1, 1994. Their movement calls for basic changes in Mexican society, including fair elections and democratic liberties for all Mexicans. Their vision "for humanity and against neoliberalism" continues to catalyze grassroots organizing worldwide.

INTRODUCTION

THE WORD AND THE SILENCE

by Greg Ruggiero

"As man perceives the extent of dehumanization, he asks himself if humanization is a viable possibility." —Paolo Freire

"The only interesting project is the liberation of everyday life." —Situationist Observation

"Why is everyone so quiet? Is this the democracy you wanted?" So ask the Zapatistas, the group of indigenous rebels who stunned the world on January 1, 1994 as they launched an insurgency movement for survival, democracy, and economic justice in their native land of Mexico.

The Zapatistas stunned the world for many reasons. First, precisely because they chose January 1, 1994, the first day of the enactment of the North American Free Trade Agreement (NAFTA), to open their brilliantly coordinated campaign against economic globalization, the Zapatistas illustrated the devastating impact that globalization can have on the fabric of local cultures. In their earliest public statements, the Zapatistas announced that NAFTA would not bring them jobs but "a death sentence." Rather than die, they organized, and fought to defend the rhythms and traditions of indigenous village life.

Secondly, during the four years of their open struggle the Zapatistas have proved that they are NOT a guerrilla force seeking to seize power, but rather a revolutionary social movement seeking to activate and mobilize "civil society"— a truly subversive project in a global economic system that seeks to place corporate interest above democratic law, and redefine citizen power as consumer choice. In situating civil society at the heart of their project, Zapatista strategies of organization and outreach provide an inspiring example of radical social empowerment and movement building for grassroots organizers, community leaders, and activists worldwide.

The Zapatista approach is revolutionary because of its emphasis on communication and dialogue over authority and force. "We are the network," say the Zapatistas, "all of us who speak and listen." This is the revolution that Paulo Freire wrote of in *Pedagogy of the Oppressed*, a revolution that seeks not only to liberate the oppressed, but the oppressors as well; an empowerment struggle lead by a vision of humanity that supports localism and diversity, and increases in power through genuine dialogue and community participation.

Speaking and listening. Consultation and deliberation. These constitute the essence of democratic process, the prerequisites to collective decision making and popular sovereignty. These strategies reveal why the Zapatista campaign has not been one of outbreaks violence, but huge, brilliantly planned, creatively executed outbreaks of *communication*. Exasperated by broken agreements and promises from the government, the Zapatista strategy has initiated the in-for-the-long-haul process of awakening and mobilizing civil society, and has succeeded through creating spaces for dialogue on every possible scale.

In their own words:

> It is the word which is the bridge to cross to the other. Silence is what the powerful offer our pain in order to make us small. When we are silenced we remain very much alone. Speaking heals the pain. Speaking we accompany one another. The powerful uses the word to impose his empire of silence. We use the word to renew ourselves. The powerful

use the silence to hide his crimes. We use silence to listen to one another, to touch one another, to know one another.

This pamphlet records the political and poetic genius of the Zapatista's largest dialogue to date, the First Intercontinental Encounter For Humanity and Against Neoliberalism which thousands of people from around the world attended in the summer of 1996. The documents presented here are the Zapatistas original invitation to international civil society to attend the Encuentro, the Zapatistas closing remarks at the end of the Encuentro, and a transcript of a video message that Subcommandante Marcos delivered a year later, elaborating the Zapatista proposal for a "decentralized intercontinental network of alternative communication."

In your hands are living words, a timely *manifesto* for resistance and revolution today. And in your hands is a *poem*, universal and timeless, expressing in Whitmanesque language the basic human urge for dignity, democracy, and liberation. As a manifesto, it marks and records the local struggle of the indigenous calling their government to justice; as poetry it marks the struggle of all people to realize our common interconnectedness despite the dehumanizing institutions of business and war.

This dual power of the Zapatista presence; the poetry of their manifestoes and the universalism of their local struggle, has situated their efforts at the heart of a global movement that represents the awakening and mobilization of civil society. The Zapatista revolution is local and global, a product of conditions in Mexico, but also the voice of humanity today. And that voice is a voice of challenge, resistance, and joy. Their tactics do not force answers, but invite *you* to ask questions of the quality of *your* own community and *your* own life. What do *you* want? Will you be a consumer or a citizen? Are you part of a market or a movement? Why is everyone so quiet? Is this the democracy you wanted?

FIRST DECLARATION OF LA REALIDAD FOR HUMANITY AND AGAINST NEOLIBERALISM

"I have arrived, I am here present, I the singer.
Enjoy in good time, come here to present your-
selves those who have a hurting heart.
I raise my song".
—Nahuatl Poetry

TO THE PEOPLE OF THE WORLD:

Brothers and Sisters:

During the last years, the power of money has presented a new mask over its criminal face. Disregarding borders, with no importance given to races or colors, the Power of money humiliates dignities, insults honesties and assassinates hopes. Re-named as "Neoliberalism", the historic crime in the concentration of privileges, wealth and impunities, democratizes misery and hopelessness.

A new world war is waged, but now against the entire humanity. As in all world wars, what is being sought is a new distribution of the world.

By the name of "globalization" they call this modern war which assassinates and forgets. The new distribution of the world consists in concentrating power in power and misery in misery.

The new distribution of the world excludes "minorities". The indigenous, youth, women, homosexuals, lesbians, people of color, immigrants, workers, peasants; the majority who make up the world basements are presented, for power, as disposable. The new distribution of the world excludes the majorities.

The modern army of financial capital and corrupt governments advance conquering in the only way it is capable of: destroying. The new distribution of the world destroys humanity.

The new distribution of the world only has one place for money and its servants. Men, women and machines become equal in servitude and in being disposable. The lie governs and it multiplies itself in means and methods.

A new lie is sold to us as history. The lie about the defeat of hope, the lie about the defeat of dignity, the lie about the defeat of humanity. The mirror of power offers us an equilibrium in the balance scale: the lie about the victory of cynicism, the lie about the victory of servitude, the lie about the victory of neoliberalism.

Instead of humanity, it offers us stock market value indexes, instead of dignity it offers us globalization of misery, instead of hope it offers us an emptiness, instead of life it offers us the international of terror.

Against the international of terror representing neoliberalism, we must raise the international of hope. Hope, above borders, languages, colors, cultures, sexes, strategies, and thoughts, of all those who prefer humanity alive.

The international of hope. Not the bureaucracy of hope, not the opposite image and, thus, the same as that which annihilates us. Not the power with a new sign or new clothing. A breath like this, the breath of dignity. A flower yes, the flower of hope. A song yes, the song of life.

Dignity is that nation without nationality, that rainbow that is also a bridge, that murmur of the heart no matter what blood lives it, that rebel irreverence that mocks borders, customs and wars.

Hope is that rejection of conformity and defeat.

Life is what they owe us: the right to govern and to govern ourselves, to think and act with a freedom that is not exercised over the slavery of others, the right to give and receive what is just.

For all this, along with those who, beyond borders, races and colors, share the song of life, the struggle against death, the flower of hope and the breath of dignity..

THE ZAPATISTA ARMY OF NATIONAL LIBERATION

Speaks...

To all who struggle for human values of democracy, liberty and justice.

To all who force themselves to resist the world crime known as "Neoliberalism" and aim for humanity and hope to be better, be synonymous of future.

To all individuals, groups, collectives, movements, social, civic and political organizations, neighborhood associations, cooperatives, all the lefts known and to be known; non-governmental organizations, groups in solidarity with struggles of the world people, bands, tribes, intellectuals, indigenous people, students, musicians, workers, artists, teachers, peasants, cultural groups, youth movements, alternative communication media, ecologists, tenants, lesbians, homosexuals, feminists, pacifists.

To all human beings without a home, without land, without work, without food, without health, without education, without freedom, without justice, without independence, without democracy, without peace, without tomorrow.

To all who, with no matter to colors, race or borders, make of hope a weapon and a shield.

And calls together to the First Intercontinental Gathering for Humanity and Against Neoliberalism.

To be celebrated between the months of April and August of 1996 in the five continents, according the following program of activities:

FIRST: Continental preparation assemblies in the month of April of 1996 in the following sites:

➤1—European Continent: Site in Berlin, Germany

➤2—American Continent: Site in La Realidad, Mexico

➤3—Asian Continent: Site in Tokyo, Japan

➤4—African Continent: Site to be defined

➤5—Oceanic Continent: Site in Sidney, Australia.

Note: The continental sites can change if the organizing groups decide to do so.

SECOND: The Intercontinental Gathering for Humanity and Against Neoliberalism, from July 27th to August 3rd of 1996, in the Zapatista "Aguascalientes", Chiapas, Mexico.

With the following Bases: Agenda:

➤Table 1—Economic aspects of how one lives under neoliberalism, how one resists, how one struggles and proposals of struggle against it and for humanity.

➤Table 2—Political aspects of how one lives under neoliberalism, how one resists, how one struggles and proposals of struggle against it and for humanity.

➤Table 3—Social aspects of how one lives under neoliberalism, how one resists, how one struggles and proposals of struggle against it and for humanity.

➤Table 4—Cultural aspects of how one lives under neoliberalism, how one resists, how one struggles and proposals of struggle against it and for humanity.

ORGANIZATION: The preparation meetings in Europe, Asia, Africa and Oceania will be organized by the Committees in Solidarity with the Zapatista Rebellion, related organisms, and citizenship groups interested in the struggle against neoliberalism and for humanity. We call upon groups of all countries so that they work united in the organization and achievement of the preparation assemblies.

The intercontinental gathering for humanity and against neoliberalism, to be celebrated from July 27th to August 3rd of 1996 in Chiapas, Mexico, will be organized by the EZLN and by citizens and Mexican non-governmental organizations that will be made known in opportune time.

ACCREDITATION: The accreditation for the preparation assemblies in the 5 continents will be made by the organizing committees formed in Europe, Asia, Africa, Oceania, and America, respectively.

The accreditations for the gathering in Chiapas, Mexico, will be done by the committees in solidarity with the Zapatista rebellion, with the people of Chiapas, and with the people of Mexico, in their respective countries; and in Mexico, by the organizing commission, which will be known in opportune time.

GENERAL AND INTERCONTINENTAL NOTE: All which has not been completed by this convocation will be resolved by the respective organizing committees regarding the continental preparation assemblies, and by the intercontinental organizing committees regarding the gathering in Chiapas, Mexico.

Brothers and Sisters:

Humanity lives in the chest of us all and, like the heart, it prefers to be on the left side. We must find it, we must find ourselves.

It is not necessary to conquer the world. It is sufficient with making it new. Us. Today.

Democracy! Liberty! Justice!

From the mountains of the Mexican Southeast.
By the Clandestine Indigenous Revolutionary
Committee General Command of the Zapatista Army
    of National Liberation.
Subcomandante Insurgente Marcos.
Mexico, January of 1996

REMARKS AT THE OPENING CEREMONY
OF THE ENCUENTRO

Brothers and Sisters
of Asia, Africa, Oceania, Europe and America:
Welcome to the mountains of the Mexican
Southeast.

Let us introduce ourselves.

We are the Zapatista National Liberation
Army. For ten years we lived in these mountains, preparing to fight a war. In these mountains we built an army.
Below, in the cities and plantations, we did
not exist. Our lives were worth less than those
of machines or animals.

We were like stones, like weeds in the road.
We were silenced. We were faceless.
We were nameless. We had no future.
We did not exist.

To the Powers that Be, known internationally by
the term "neoliberalism," we did not count, we
did not produce, we did not buy, we did not sell.
We were a cipher in the accounts of big capital.

Then we went to the mountains to find ourselves and see if we could ease the pain of being forgotten stones and weeds.

Here, in the mountains of Southeastern Mexico, our dead live on.

Our dead, who live in the mountains, know many things.

They speak to us of their death, and we hear them.

Coffins speak and tell us another story that comes from yesterday and points toward tomorrow. The mountains spoke to us, the Macehualob, the common and ordinary people.

We are simple people, as the Powerful tell us.

Every day and the next night, the powerful want us to dance the X-tol and repeat their brutal conquest. The Kaz-Dzul, the false man, rules our lands and has giant war machines, like the Boob, half-puma and half-horse, that spread pain and death among us.

The trickster government sends us theAluxob, the liars who fool our people and make them forgetful.

This is why we became soldiers.
This is why we remain soldiers:
   because we want no more death and trickery for our people,
   because we want no more forgetting.

The mountain told us to take up arms so we would have a voice.
   It told us to cover our faces so we would have a face.
   It told us to forget our names so we could be named.
   It told us to protect our past so we would have a future.

In the mountains the dead live: our dead.

With them live the Votán and the Ikál,
   the light and the darkness, the wet and the dry,
   the earth and the wind, the rain and the fire.

The mountain is the home of the Halach Uinic,

the true people, the true leader. Here we learned and remembered that we are what we are,

the real men and women.

So, with our voice strengthening our hands, with our face reborn, with our name renamed, our yesterday at the center of the four points of Chan Santa Cruz in Balam Ná, the star was born that defines humanity and reminds us that there are five parts that make up the world.

In the season when the Chaacob ride, spreading the rain, we came down once more to speak with our own and prepare the storm that will signal the harvest.

We brought forth the war in the year zero, and we began to walk this path that has brought us to your hearts and today brings you to ours.

This is who we are. The Zapatista National Liberation Army.

The voice that arms itself to be heard,
the face that hides itself to be seen,
the name that hides itself to be named,
the red star that calls out to humanity around

the world to be heard, to be seen, to be named.
the tomorrow that is harvested in the past.

Behind our black mask,
behind our armed voice,
behind our unnameable name,
behind what you see of us,
behind this, we are you.
behind this, we are the same simple and ordinary men and women who are repeated in all races, painted in all colors, speak in all languages and live in all places.

Behind this, we are the same forgotten men and women,
the same excluded, the same untolerated,
the same persecuted, the same as you.

Behind this, we are you.

Behind our masks is the face of all excluded women,
of all the forgotten native people,
of all the persecuted homosexuals,
of all the despised youth,
of all the beaten migrants,
of all those imprisoned for their words and

thoughts,
    of all the humiliated workers,
    of all those dead from neglect,
    of all the simple and ordinary men and
women
        who don't count,
        who aren't seen,
        who are nameless,
        who have no tomorrow.

Brothers and Sisters:
    We have invited you to this meeting to
seek and to find yourselves and us.

You have all touched our heart, and you can see
we are not special.

You can see we are simple and ordinary men
and women.

You can see we are the rebellious mirror that
wants to be a pane of glass and break.

You can see we are who we are so we can stop
being who we are
    to become the you who we are.

We are the Zapatistas.

We invited you for all of us to hear ourselves
and speak to ourselves,
to see all that we are.

Brothers and Sisters:
    In these mountains, the talking coffins
spoke to us and told us ancient stories that
recall our pains and our rebellions.

Our dreams will not end as long as we live.

We will not give up our banner.

Our death will live on forever.
    So say the mountains who speak to us.
    So says the star who shines in Chan Santa
Cruz.

She tells us that the Cruzob,[10] the rebels, will
not be defeated and will continue on their road
along with all those in the human constellation.

The red star who will help the world be free
tells us that the red people, the Chachac-Mac,[11]
will always come.

The star who is the mountains tells us,
    that a people is five peoples,
    that a people who are a star are all people,
    that the people who are humanity are all
the world's people.

They will come to aid the worlds who become
people in their struggle.

So the real man and woman live without pain
and the hearts of stone are melted.

You are all the Chachac-Mac, the people who
come to help the man of five parts throughout
the world,
    among all peoples, in all nations.

You are all the red star who mirrors us.

We can continue on the right path if we, the
you who are us, walk together.

Brothers and Sisters:
    Among our peoples, the oldest sages have
put a cross that is a star where the water, the
giver of life, is born.

Thus, a star marks the beginning of life in the mountains.

Thus are born the streams that come down from the mountain and raise the voice of the speaking star of our Chan Santa Cruz.

The voice of the mountain has spoken, saying that the real men and women will live free
    when they give themselves to the five-pointed star,
    when the five peoples make themselves one in the star,
    when the five parts of humanity who are the world find themselves and find each other,
    when all five find their place and the place of each other.

Today, thousands of different roads that come from the five continents meet here in the mountains of the Mexican Southeast, to join their steps.

Today, thousands of words from the five continents are silent here in the mountains of the Mexican Southeast, to hear each other and hear themselves.

Today, thousands of struggles from the five continents struggle here in the mountains of the Mexican Southeast, for life and against death.

Today, thousands of colors from the five continents are painted here in the mountains of the Mexican Southeast,
to announce a future of inclusion and tolerance.

Today, thousands of hearts from the five continents are alive here in the mountains of the Mexican Southeast,
for humanity and against neoliberalism.

Today, thousands of human beings from the five continents shout "enough" here in the mountains of the Mexican Southeast,
enough of conformity, of doing nothing, of cynicism, of egoism, the modern god.

Today, thousands of small worlds from the five continents are attempting a beginning here in the mountains of the Mexican Southeast,
the beginning of the construction of a new and good world,

that is, a world which admits all these worlds.

Today, thousands of men and women of the five continents begin here in the mountains of the Mexican Southeast,
the First Intercontinental Meeting For Humanity and Against Neoliberalism.

Brothers and Sisters of the entire world:
Welcome to the mountains of the Mexican Southeast.
Welcome to this corner of the world where we are all the same because we are different.
Welcome to the search for life and the struggle against death.
Welcome to this First Intercontinental Meeting For Humanity and Against Neoliberalism.

Democracy! Freedom! Justice!

From the mountains of the Mexican Southeast.
The Indigenous Revolutionary Clandestine Committee—General Command Zapatista Army of National Liberation.
La Realidad (Reality), Planet Earth, August, 1996.

Translation source: "Dark Night field notes" No. 8/9: winter/spring 1997, published by Dark Night Press, P.O. Box 3629, Chicago, IL 60690-3629; darknight@igc.apc.org

2ND DECLARATION OF LA REALIDAD

CLOSING WORDS OF THE EZLN AT THE INTERCONTINENTAL ENCUENTRO FOR HUMANITY AND AGAINST NEOLIBERALISM

First read by Subcomandante Marcos August 3, 1996.

Through my voice speaks the voice of the Zapatista Army of National Liberation

Brothers and sisters of the whole world: Brothers and sisters of Africa, America, Asia, Europe, and Oceania:

Brothers and sisters attending the First Intercontinental Encounter for Humanity and Against Neoliberalism:
Welcome to the Zapatista R/reality.

Welcome to this territory in struggle for humanity. Welcome to this territory in rebellion against neoliberalism.

The Zapatistas greet all who attended this encounter. Here, in the mountains of the Mexican Southeast, when an assembly greets whoever comes with good words, we applaud. We ask that everyone greet each other and that everyone greet the delegations from: Italy, Brazil, Great Britain, Paraguay, Chile, the Philippines, Germany, Peru, Argentina, Austria, Uruguay, Guatemala, Belgium, Venezuela, Iran, Denmark, Nicaragua, Zaire, France, Haiti, Ecuador, Greece, Japan, Kurdistan, Ireland, Costa Rica, Cuba, Sweden, the Netherlands, South Africa, Switzerland, Spain, Portugal, the United States, the Basque country, Turkey, Canada, Puerto Rico, Bolivia, Australia, Mauritania, Mexico [Norway and Colombia are called out from the crowd].

Welcome, all men, women, children, and elders from the five continents who have responded to the invitation of the Zapatista indigenous to search for hope, for humanity, and to struggle against neoliberalism.

Brothers and sisters:

When this dream that awakens today in R/reality began to be dreamed by us, we thought it would be a failure.

We thought that, maybe, we could gather a few dozen people here from a handful of countries.

We were wrong. As always, we were wrong.

It wasn't a few dozen, but thousands of human beings, those who came from the five continents to find themselves in R/reality at the close of the twentieth century.

The word born within these mountains, these Zapatista mountains, found the ears of those who could hear, care for and launch it anew, so that it might travel far away and circle the world.

The sheer lunacy of convoking the five continents to reflect clearly on our past, our present, and our future, found that it wasn't alone in its delirium. Soon lunacies from the whole planet began to work on bringing the dream to R/reality,

to bathe it in the mud,
grow it in the rain,
moisten it in the sun,
speak it with each other,
bring it forth,
giving it shape and substance.

As to what happened in these days, much will be written later.

Today we can say that we are certain of at least one thing: A dream dreamed in the five continents can realize itself in R/reality.

Who now will be able to tell us that dreaming is lovely but futile?

Who now will be able to argue that dreams, however many the dreamers, cannot become a reality?

How is joy dreamed in Africa?

What marvels walk in the European dream?
How many tomorrows does the dream encompass in Asia?

To what music does the American dream dance?

How does the heart speak that dreams in Oceania?

To whom does it matter how and what we dream here or in any part of the world?

Who are they who dare to let their dreams meet with all the dreams of the world?

What's happening in the mountains of the Mexican Southeast that finds an echo and a mirror

in the streets of Europe,
the suburbs of Asia,
the countryside of America,
the townships of Africa,
and the houses of Oceania?

What's happening with the peoples of these five continents who, so we are all told, only encounter each other to compete or make war?

Wasn't this turn of the century synonymous with despair, bitterness, and cynicism?

From where and how did all these dreams come to R/reality?

May Europe speak and recount the long bridge of its gaze crossing the Atlantic and history coming to rediscover itself in R/reality.

May Asia speak and explain the gigantic leap of its heart coming to beat in R/reality.

May Africa speak and describe the long sailing of its restless image coming to reflect upon itself in R/reality.

May Oceania speak and tell of the many flights of its thought   coming to rest in R/reality.

May America speak and remember its swelling hope coming to renew itself in R/reality.

May the five continents speak and everyone listen.

May humanity suspend for a moment its silence of shame and anguish.

May humanity speak.

May humanity listen....

In the world of those who live in the Power and kill for the Power, the human being wasn't fit.

There is no space for hope, no place for tomorrow.

Slavery or death is the choice that their world offers all worlds.

The world of money, their world, governs from the stock exchanges. Today, speculation is the principal source of enrichment and, at the same time, the best demonstration of the atrophy of human beings capacity to work. Work is no longer necessary in order to produce wealth; now all that's needed is speculation. Crimes and wars are carried out so that the global stock exchanges may be pillaged by one or the other.

Meanwhile, millions of women, millions of youths,
    millions of indigenous,
    millions of homosexuals,
    millions of human beings of all races and colors participate in the financial markets only as a devalued currency, always worth less and less, the currency of their blood turning a profit.

The globalization of markets erases borders for speculation and crime and multiplies them for human beings. Countries are obliged to erase their national borders for money to circulate, but to multiply their internal borders.

Neoliberalism wasn't turn many countries into one country, it turns each country into many countries.

The lie of unipolarity and internationalization turns itself into a nightmare of war, a fragmented war, again and again, so many times that nations are pulverized.

In this world the Power globalizes to overcome the obstacles to its war of conquest.

National governments are turned into the military underlings of a new world war against humanity.

From the stupid course of nuclear armament, destined to annihilate humanity in one blow, it has turned to the absurd militarization of every aspect in the life of national societies, a militarization destined to annihilate humanity in many blows, in many places, and in many ways. What were formerly known as "national armies" are turning into mere units of a greater army, one that neoliberalism arms to lead against humanity. The end of the so-called "Cold War" didn't stop the global arms race, it only changed the model for the merchandising of mortality: weapons of all kinds and sizes for all kinds of criminal tastes. More and more, not only are the so-called "institutional" armies armed, but also the armies drug trafficking builds up to assure its reign. More or less rapidly, national societies are being militarized and armies, supposedly created to protect their borders from foreign enemies, are turning their cannons and rifles around and aiming them inward.

It is not possible for neoliberalism to become the world's reality

without the argument of death served up by

institutional and private armies,
       without the gag served up by prisons,
       without the blows and assassinations served
up by the military and the police.

National repression is a necessary premise of the
globalization neoliberalism imposes.
       The more neoliberalism advances as a global
system, the more numerous grow the weapons
and the ranks of the armies and national police.
       The numbers of the imprisoned, the disap-
peared, and the assassinated in different countries
also grows.

A world war: the most brutal,
       the most complete,
       the most universal,
       the most effective.

Each country,
       each city,
       each countryside,
       each house,
       each person:
       each is a large or small battleground.

On the one side is neoliberalism with all its

repressive power and all its machinery of death;

On the other side is the human being.

There are those who resign themselves to being one more number in the huge *bolsa*—bag, pocket, or stock exchange—of Power. There are those who resign themselves to being slaves. He who is himself master to slaves also cynically walks the slave's horizontal ladder.

In exchange for the bad life and crumbs that Power hands out, there are those who sell themselves,
    resign themselves,
    surrender themselves.

In any part of the world, there are slaves who say they are happy being slaves.

In any part of the world, there are men and women who stop being human and take their place in the gigantic market that trades in dignities.

But there are those who do not resign themselves,
    there are those who decide to be awkward,
    there are those who do not sell themselves,

there are those who do not surrender themselves.

There are, around the world, those who resist being annihilated in this war. There are those who decide to fight.

In any place in the world, anytime, any man or any woman rebels to the point of tearing off the clothes resignation has woven for them and cynicism has dyed gray.

Any man, any woman, of whatever color, in whatever tongue, speaks and says to himself, to herself, "Enough is enough!"—*Ya Basta!*

Enough is enough of lies.
Enough is enough of crime.
Enough is enough of death.

"Enough is enough of war," any man, any woman, says to himself, herself.

In whatever part of any of the five continents any man, any woman, eagerly resists the Power and constructs his own, her own path that wasn't lead to the loss of dignity and hope.

Any man or any woman decides to live and struggle for his part, her part in history. No longer does the Power dictate his steps, her steps; no longer does the Power administer life and decide death.

Any man or any woman responds to death with life, and responds to the nightmare by dreaming and struggling against war, against neoliberalism, for humanity....

For struggling for a better world all of us are fenced in, threatened with death.

The fence is reproduced globally.

In every continent,
    every city,
    every countryside,
    every house.

The Power s fence of war closes in on the rebels, the rebels whom humanity always thanks.

But fences are broken. In every house,
    in every countryside,
    in every city,

in every state,
in every country,
on every continent
the rebels, whom human history throws up along
its whole course to assure itself of hope, struggle
and the fence breaks.

The rebels search each other out.

They walk towards one another.

They find each other and together break other
fences.

In the countryside and cities, in the states, in the
nations, on the continents, the rebels begin to rec-
ognize themselves, to know themselves equal and
different.

They continue on their fatiguing walk, walking
as it is now necessary to walk, that is to say,
struggling....

A R/reality spoke to them then.
Rebels from the five continents heard it and set
off walking.

To arrive at the intercontinental R/reality, each one has had to make his own, her own path. From the five arms of the star of the world, the step of men and women, whose dignified word searched for a place to be spoken and heard, has come to R/reality, the place of the encounter. It was necessary to break through many fences to come and break through the fence around R/reality.

There are different fences. In ours, one must get past the police, customs officials, tanks, cannons, trenches, planes, helicopters, rain, mud, insects.

Each one of the rebels from the five continents has his own, her own fence, struggle, and a broken fence to add to the memory of other rebels.

So it was that this intercontinental encounter began. It was initiated on all the continents, in all the countries, in all the places where any man or any woman began to speak and say to themselves, "Enough is enough!"

Who can say in what precise locale and at what exact hour and date this intercontinental encounter for humanity and against neoliberalism began? We don't know. But we do know who initiated it.

All the rebels around the world started it.

Here, we are only a small part of those rebels, it's true. But to all the diverse fences that all the rebels of the world break every day, you have added one more rupture, that of the fence around the Zapatista R/reality.

To achieve that, you had to struggle against your respective governments and then confront the fence of papers and procedures with which the Mexican government thought to detain you. You are all fighters, men and women who break through fences of all kinds. That s why you made it to R/reality. Maybe you can t yet see the greatness of your achievement, but we see it.

* * *

Some of the best rebels from the five continents arrived in the mountains of the Mexican Southeast. All of them brought their ideas, their hearts, their worlds. To find themselves among other ideas, other reasons, other worlds for that they came to R/reality.

A world made of many worlds found itself these days in the mountains of the Mexican Southeast.

A world made of many worlds opened a space

and established its right to be possible, raised the banner of being necessary, fastened to the middle of the earth's R/reality to announce a better future.

A world of all the worlds that rebel and resist the Power,

a world of all the worlds that inhabit this world opposing cynicism,
a world that struggles for humanity and against neoliberalism.

This was the world that we lived these days.

This is the world that we found here....

This encounter doesn't end in R/reality.

It just so happens that now it must search for a place to carry on.

But what next?

A new number in the useless enumeration of the numerous international orders?

A new scheme for calming and easing the anguish of having no recipe?

A global program for world revolution?

A utopian theory so that it can maintain a prudent distance from the reality that anguishes us?

An "organigram" that assures each of us a position, a task, a title, and no work?

An echo that reechoes, a reflected image of the possible and forgotten: the possibility and necessity of speaking and listening.

Not an echo that peters out or a force that decreases after reaching its apogee. An echo that breaks barriers and reechoes.

An echo of small magnitude, the local and particular, reverberating in the echo of great magnitude, the intercontinental and galactic.

An echo that recognizes the existence of the other and does not overpower or attempt to silence it.

An echo that takes its place and speaks its own voice yet speaks the voice of the other.

An echo that reproduces its own sound yet opens itself to the sound of the other.

An echo of this rebel voice transforming itself and renewing itself in other voices.

An echo that turns itself into many voices, into a network of voices that, before the deafness of the Power, opts to speak to itself,
knowing itself to be one and many,
acknowledging itself to be equal in its desire to listen and be listened to,
recognizing itself as diverse in the tones and levels of voices forming it.

A network of voices that resist the war the Power wages on them.

A network of voices that not only speak, but also struggle and resist for humanity and against neoliberalism.

A network of voices that are born resisting, reproducing their resistance in quieter or lonelier voices.

A network that covers the five continents and helps to resist the death that Power promises us.

A great *bolsa* of voices, sounds that search for their place, fitting in with others, continues.

A great torn *bolsa*, that keeps the best of itself yet opens itself to what's better, continues.

A pocket mirror of voices,
     the world in which sounds may be listened to separately, recognizing their specificity,
     the world in which sounds may include themselves in one great sound, continues.

The reproduction of resistances, the "I am not resigned," the "I am a rebel," continues.

The world with the many worlds that the world needs, continues.

Humanity, recognizing itself to be plural, different, inclusive, tolerant of itself, in hope, continues.

The human and rebel voice, consulted on the five continents in order to become a network of voices and resistance, continues.

The voice of all the people we are, the voice that speaks this Second Declaration of Reality for Humanity and Against Neoliberalism, continues.

Brothers and sisters of Africa, Asia, America, Europe, and Oceania:

CONSIDERING THAT WE ARE:
Against the international order of death,
    against the globalization of war and armaments.

Against dictatorships,
    against authoritarianism,
    against repression.

Against the politics of economic liberalization,
    against hunger,
    against poverty,
    against robbery,
    against corruption.

Against patriarchy,
    against xenophobia,
    against discrimination,
    against racism,

against crime,
against the destruction of the environment,
against militarism.

Against stupidity,
against lies,
against ignorance.

Against slavery,
against intolerance,
against injustice,
against marginalization,
against forgetfulness.

Against neoliberalism.

CONSIDERING THAT WE ARE:
For the international order of hope,
for a new, just, and dignified peace.

For a new politics,
for democracy,
for political liberties.

For justice,
for life, and dignified work.

For civil society,
> for full rights for women in every regard,
> for respect for elders, youth, and children,
> for the defense and protection of the environment.

For intelligence,
> for culture,
> for education,
> for truth.

For liberty,
> for tolerance,
> for inclusion,
> for remembrance.

For humanity.

WE DECLARE:
First

That we will make a collective network of all our particular struggles and resistances. An intercontinental network of resistance against neoliberalism, an intercontinental network of resistance for humanity.

This intercontinental network of resistance, recognizing differences and acknowledging similarities, will strive to find itself in other resistances around the world. This intercontinental network of resistance will be the medium in which distinct resistances may support one another. This intercontinental network of resistance is not an organizing structure; it wasn't have a central head or decision maker; it has no central command or hierarchies. We are the network, all of us who resist.

Second

That we will make a network of communication among all our struggles and resistances. An intercontinental network of alternative communication against neoliberalism, an intercontinental network of alternative communication for humanity.

This intercontinental network of alternative communication will search to weave channels so that words may travel all the paths that resist. This intercontinental network of alternative communication will be the medium by which distinct resistances communicate with one another.

This intercontinental network of alternative communication is not an organizing structure, nor does it have a central head or decision maker, nor does it have a central command or hierarchies. We are the network, all of us who speak and listen.

THIS WE DECLARE:

To speak and to listen for humanity and against neoliberalism.

To resist and struggle for humanity and against neoliberalism.

For the whole world: Democracy! Liberty! Justice!

From whatever reality of whichever continent!

Brothers and sisters:

We do not propose that those of us who are present here sign this declaration and end this Encuentro today. We propose that the Intercontinental Encounter for Humanity and Against Neoliberalism continue on every continent, in every country, in every countryside and city, in every house, school or workplace where human beings live who want a better world.

The indigenous communities have taught us

that to resolve a problem, no matter how great it may be, it is always good to consult all of the people we are. That is why we propose that this declaration be distributed around the world and that a consultation be carried out, at least in all the countries in attendance, on the following question:

Do you agree to subscribe to the Second Declaration of Reality, for Humanity, and Against Neoliberalism?

We propose that this Intercontinental Consultation for Humanity and Against Neoliberalism be realized on the five continents during the first two weeks of December 1996.

We propose that we organize this Consultation in the same way that this Encuentro was organized, that all of us who attended and those who couldn't but who followed us from afar in this Encuentro, organize and carry out the Consultation. We propose that we make use of all possible and impossible media in order to consult with the greatest number of human beings on the five continents. The Intercontinental Consultation is part of the resistance we are organizing and one way of making contacts and encounters with other resistances. Part of a new way of doing political work in the world, that is what the Intercontinental Consultation wants to be.

Not only that. We also propose that we now call people to the Second Intercontinental Encounter for Humanity and Against Neoliberalism.

We propose that it be carried out in the second half of 1997 and that it be in the European continent.* We propose that the exact date and place of the Encuentro be defined by the brothers and sisters of Europe in a meeting they hold after this first Encuentro.

We all hope that there will be this Second Intercontinental Encounter and that it be held, of course, on another continent. When this Second Encounter is held, we want to make it clear from this moment on that we will find a way to participate directly, wherever it is held.

BROTHERS AND SISTERS:

We continue to be awkward.

---

* The 1997 European Encuentro convened in Barcelona, Spain from July 26 to August 2, 1997. As during the 1996 Encuentro in Chiapas, there were five venues. There also were common opening and closing meetings, with the main event taking place in Spain.

　　　　　　　　THE ZAPATISTAS

What the theorists of neoliberalism tell us is false: that everything is under control, including everything that isn't under control.

We are not a safety valve* for the rebellion that could destabilize neoliberalism.

It is false that our rebel existence legitimates the Power.

The Power fears us.

That is why it pursues us and fences us in.

That is why it jails and kills us.

In R/reality, we are the possibility that it can be defeated and made to disappear.

Maybe there are not so many of us, but we are men and women who struggle for humanity,
    who struggle against neoliberalism.

We are men and women who struggle around the

---

* "Safety valve," here refers to a long history of characteristically short-sighted and short-term "solutions" on the part of the Mexican government in response to immediate popular pressure.

world. We are men and women who want the five continents to have:

Democracy! Liberty! Justice!

From the mountains of the Mexican Southeast.
The Indigenous Revolutionary Clandestine Committee—General Command Zapatista Army of National Liberation.
La Realidad (Reality), Planet Earth, August, 1996.

Translation source: "Dark Night field notes" No. 8/9: winter/spring 1997, published by Dark Night Press, P.O. Box 3629, Chicago, IL 60690-3629; darknight@igc.apc.org

SUBCOMMANDANTE MARCOS'S MESSAGE TO "FREEING THE MEDIA" TEACH-IN, NYC JANUARY 1997

Translation of a 10-minute video message made in La Realidad, January 1997.

We are in the mountains of Southeast Mexico in the Lacandon Jungle of Chiapas and we want to use this medium with the help of the National Commission for Democracy in Mexico, to send a greeting to the "Freeing the Media" Conference that is taking place in New York, where there are brothers and sisters of independent communication media from the US and Canada.

At the Intercontinental Encounter for Humanity and Against Neoliberalism we said: A global decomposition is taking place, we call it the Fourth World War*—neoliberalism: the global economic process to eliminate that multitude of people who are not useful to the powerful—the groups called "minorities" in the mathematics of power, but who happen to be the majority population in the world. We find ourselves in a world system of globalization willing to sacrifice millions of human beings.

---

* The Zapatistas see the Cold War as the Third World War, and economic globalization or Neoliberlaism, as the Fourth World War.

The giant communication media: the great monsters of the television industry, the communication satellites, magazines, and newspapers seem determined to present a virtual world, created in the image of what the globalization process requires.

In this sense, the world of contemporary news is a world that exists for the VIP's—the very important people. Their everyday lives are what is important: if they get married, if they divorce, if they eat, what clothes they wear and what clothes they take off—these major movie stars and big politicians. But common people only appear for a moment—when they kill someone, or when they die. For the communication giants and the neoliberal powers, the others, the excluded, only exist when they are dead, or when they are in jail or court. This can't go on. Sooner or later this virtual world clashes with the real world. And that is actually happening: this clash produces results of rebellion and war throughout the entire world, or what is left of the world to even have war.

We have a choice: we can have a cynical attitude in the face of the media, to say that nothing can be done about the dollar power that creates itself in images, words, digital communication, and computer systems that invades not just with an invasion of power, but with a way of seeing that world, of how they think the world should look. We could say, well, "that's the way it is" and do nothing. Or we can simply assume incredulity: we can say that any communication by the media monopolies is a total lie. We can ignore it and go about our lives.

But there is a third option that is neither conformity, nor skepticism, nor distrust: that is to construct a different way—to show the world what is really happening—to have a critical world view and to become interested in the truth of what happens to the people who inhabit every corner of this world.

The work of independent media is to tell the history of social struggle in the world, and here in North America—the US, Canada and Mexico, independent media has, on occasion, been able to open spaces even within the mass media monopolies: to force them to acknowledge news of other social movements.

The problem is not only to know what is occurring in the world, but to understand it and to derive lessons from it—just as if we were studying history—a history not of the past, but a history of what is happening at any given moment in whatever part of the world. This is the way to learn who we are, what it is we want, who we can be and what we can do or not do.

By not having to answer to the monster media monopolies, the independent media has a life work, a political project and purpose: to let the truth be known. This is more and more important in the globalization process. This truth becomes a knot of resistance against the lie. It is our only possibility to save the truth, to maintain it, and distribute it, little by little, just as the books were saved in *Fahrenheit 451*—in which a group of people dedicated themselves to memorize books, to save them from being destroyed, so that the ideas would not be lost.

This same way, independent media tries to save history: the present history—saving it and trying to share it, so it will not disappear, moreover to distribute it to other places, so that this history is not limited to one country, to one region, to one city or social group. It is necessary not only for independent voices to exchange information and to broaden the channels, but to resist the spreading lies of the monopolies. The truth that we build in our groups, our cities, our regions, our countries, will reach full potential if we join with other truths and realize that what is occurring in other parts of the world also is part of human history.

In August 1996, we called for the creation of a network of independent media, a network of information. We mean a network to resist the power of the lie that sells us this war that we call the Fourth World War. We need this network not only as a tool for our social movements, but for our lives: this is a project of life, of humanity, humanity which has a right to critical and truthful information.

We greet all of you, recognizing the work you have done so that the struggle of indigenous people is known, and that other struggles are known, so that the great events of this world are seen in a critical form. We hope your meeting is a success and that it results in concrete plans for this network, these exchanges, this mutual support that should exist between cultural workers and independent media makers. We hope that one day we can personally attend your meeting, or perhaps that one day you can have your conference in our territory, so we can listen to your words and you can hear ours in person. For now, well, we take advantage of the help of the National Commission for Democracy in Mexico to use this video to send a greeting. [This section in English:] I don't know if my English is OK but good luck and so long. Cut.

MORE INFORMATION

NATIONAL COMMISSION FOR
DEMOCRACY IN MEXICO
5902 Monterey Rd., #194
Los Angeles, CA 90042
Phone: 213-254-9550
New toll free:1-800-405-7770
Fax: 213-254-9597
moonlight@igc.apc.or
http://www.igc.apc.org/ncdm/index.html

EZLN (Zapatista)
http://www.ezln.org/

ZAPATISTA FRONT OF NATIONAL
LIBERATION
http://www.peak.org/~joshua/fzln/

2ND ENCUENTRO FOR HUMANITY AND
AGAINST NEOLIBERALISM
http://www.geocities.com/CapitolHill/3849/ gath-
erdx.html

ACCION ZAPATISTA
http://www.utexas.edu/ftp/student/nave/

SOLIDARITY PAGES WITH MEXICO
http://www.geocities.com/CapitolHill/3102/